FREE MONEY FOR STUDENT LOANS:

A Step-by-Step Proven Strategy to
Pay off Your Debt in Four Years or Less

FREE MONEY FOR STUDENT LOANS:

A Step-by-Step Proven Strategy to Pay off Your Debt in Four Years or Less

---

1ST EDITION

STEPHEN ATHERHOLT

ISBN-10: 1547155175
ISBN-13: 978-1547155170

Dedication:

This book is dedicated to the love of my life. Thank you, Jessica, for always believing in me even when I doubted myself. Thank you for your love, support, and for so many grand adventures. You are my hero.

CONTENTS

1 THE RIVER

Money is like a river. It flows from person to person, carving a path across the land. Money, like water, sustains our lives. It provides food, housing, and transportation. We build our lives around the river knowing that without it, our lives cannot continue. But the river is immensely powerful and has dangerous currents that can carry you away. Most people have no idea how to navigate this tremulous river. They either stand at the shore afraid of its current, or like most people, they jump in with no idea how to swim. The current of money flips them over and over, tumbling them downstream into more and more debt. A few people learn to swim the river of money and make their way to shore. The rest feel so overwhelmed by the force of the river that they give up and let it carry them downstream and finally dump them over the waterfall. The power of the waterfall is devastating and most people give up all hope.

But what if there is a way to change the flow in the river of money? What if there is another current that carries you upstream? This channel reverses the flow of money and gives you control over its direction. Your journey is about to shift, and although it's much harder to swim upstream, the end result is so worth it.

Welcome to your new life. This book is the beginning of your journey. Read it, cover to cover. There may be times this journey sounds too hard for you, but read it anyway. There are so many tools in this book that you're sure to find some nuggets of truth to apply.

So where did this book come from? It came from my story. I came out of college with $65,000 in student loan debt. I never made more than $35,000 per year at my primary job, and after taxes and insurance, I brought home $25,000 per year. With that $25,000 I had to pay for my car, housing, utilities, food, bills, and my student loan. But after learning how to find "free money" I was able to pay off $75,000 ($65,000 principal and $10,000 in interest) in student loans in just 3 and ½ years.

But this book isn't about me; it's about you. So how do *you* pay off your debt quickly? Well, it won't be easy. But I've tried to make reading this book easy. My intention is to keep it simple, straightforward, informative, and interesting. My hope for all of my readers is to change their mindset about money, give them a core plan to change their finances, and help them pay off their student debt in four years or less. Some of you will take longer, but most of you can pay off your loans in three, two, or even one year. If you realize it will take longer, don't give up. Focus on the tools in this book, and apply them one by one. Once you begin to see change I guarantee it will inspire you. Oh, and hopefully you bought this book used or as an EBook so you could save money. After all, saving money is a pretty important part of this book's heart. Let's do this.

"When I was young I thought that money was the most important thing in life; now that I am old I know that it is." - Oscar Wilde

2 GRADUATION

When I graduated from high school, I dreamt of becoming an actor. Hollywood was calling my name ...or at least a small role on Broadway. In reality, New York and Los Angeles are overflowing with out-of-work actors, but don't tell that to my 18-year-old self. I wasn't a bad-looking guy and had a mediocre level of talent, but I wasn't quite ready for the big leagues. College seemed to be the next logical step. Shopping for college seemed fairly simple, find a good program that would accept me. It wasn't until later that I realized this would be one of the most expensive purchases I would ever make in my life, with little to no knowledge of what I was doing. My parents didn't have much to say, and my school counselor was more interested in Golf Digest than in me.

So I began to shop. Looking for colleges is a bit like window-shopping in front of *Tiffany's* for a $100,000 piece of jewelry that you don't get to keep after you buy. You may learn something from the exchange, but the money is gone. So that's what I did. I bought $100,000 worth of education over the next 7 years. Thankfully I had some scholarships, so my total school debt was a mere $65,000. (Excuse me while I vomit a little.)

Fast forward to graduation. I'm a trained actor ready to take on the world. New York and LA have no idea what's about to hit them. Then again, neither do I. As I race off to New York, my first student loan bill gathers momentum. It shoots out of the cannon of collectors at seven hundred miles per hour. Translation: I had to pay them $700 a month for the next 12 years of my life. That realization hit me right in the stomach, and I doubled over with anxiety. Do you have any idea how expensive it is to live in New York and LA? The average apartment in LA rents for $2,000 per month, and in New York the average is over $3,000 per month. Life suddenly became more expensive than I could manage. Even if I split rent with roommates and ate rock soup, I couldn't afford another $700 per month on top of my other expenses. Moving back in with Mom and Dad wasn't an option for me, so I had to give up on my goal of stardom for a time and find a more stable job.

Well lucky for me, I found a theater job that hired for the entire year and offered a salaried position as well as benefits. This is unheard of in the acting community. Now I was on track to pay off my school debt . . . over the next 12 years. That meant there were 12 years of school debt between my dreams and me. By the time I paid them off, I would be in my late 30s, and my chance of acting success would be long gone. My heart began to race, and the walls started closing in. I was trapped, with no easy way out. I started looking for government programs, online financial help sites - anything that would get me out of paying the crushing debt. It's funny; if you rack up $65,000 in credit card debt you can get the total reduced through programs, get some of it forgiven, or in the worst case, you can file for bankruptcy and have it all wiped away. Granted, the process is horrible and devastating and recent laws have made it much harder to do. Still, there are options for irresponsible credit card spending, but none for school debt.

I knew there had to be a way to get past these loans, maybe

change the payment plan to 30 years? It would decrease the payments to $450 a month. Well, that would suck even more. Thirty years of paying down my school debt? Somebody please help me! But there are no get-out-of-debt quick programs or government aid. You can't file bankruptcy for student loans. I felt so alone . . . but I wasn't.

"Very few people can afford to be poor." - George Bernard Shaw

3 YOU ARE NOT ALONE

First, you have to realize that you're not alone. Student loan debt is a pandemic in the United States as school cost increases dramatically and financial aid decreases just as drastically. Tuition cost has increased beyond 130% over the past 20 years, and people are borrowing over twice what they did a decade ago because grants and scholarships just can't keep up. Our generation is the first in history projected to still be paying our student loans when our children go to college. That is truly disturbing. *US News and World Reports* stated, "[...] the average 2016 grad holds $37,172 in student debt . . . and a recent Citizen's Bank survey finds 59 percent of millennial graduates say they have no idea when their student loans will be paid off." Many of you will scoff at that number because your student loans are 2, 3, or even 4 times that amount. That is the average, so for all of the lucky ones who have help paying for college, the rest of us have $60,000 or more. School debt has recently eclipsed credit card debt. As of 2017, the national student loan total has reached a staggering 1.5 trillion dollars. If you're a visual person the total looks like this: $1,500,000,000,000. *YOU ARE NOT ALONE.*

"For every minute spent organizing, an hour is earned." - Benjamin Franklin

4 GET THINGS IN ORDER

The challenge now is to step out of the mass of financial mess and put yourself on the path to paying off your student loans fast! Before you tackle the hard stuff, you'll want to get your student loans organized. If you have multiple loans, you may want to consolidate them. The primary advantage of consolidation is you only have to pay one bill per month. You may also be able to reduce your monthly payment, but keep in mind that a lower monthly payment means extra years to pay it off. We will go over this strategy in greater detail later. There are a few rules to abide by when consolidating:

1. Search around for different options before consolidating. You may find a lower rate with different banks, institutions, or programs.

2. Consolidate everything if your loans have a higher interest rate than the consolidated rate.

3. If you have a subsidized loan that gives you a really low interest rate, you won't want to consolidate that loan into a

higher interest loan. Let's say you have a state supported loan at 3% interest. You also have two other loans at 8% interest. If you find a loan consolidation at 6.5%, it makes sense to merge the two higher interest loans and leave the state supported loan separate. You will then pay off the higher interest loan first because it is costing you more on a daily basis.

4. Federal loans and private loans differ with consolidation. Federal loans are pretty easy to consolidate. You can go to LoanConsolidation.ed.gov to get more information. The government puts a maximum on the interest rate. It is also a fixed rate and will remain the same throughout the life of the loan.

5. Private loans are usually a variable rate. This is great if the interest rates are low, but when the rates climb, it could be very bad. They are also harder to consolidate because you have to meet the bank's criteria. If you just graduated from college, you may not have a sufficient credit score to consolidate your private loans. The bank will require a cosigner. If someone is willing to co-sign a consolidation for you, make sure that you ask for a release in the agreement. This allows the cosigner to fall off the loan after a set amount of time. For instance, as long as you pay on time for 12 months, the cosigner is taken off the loan agreement.

6. You can only consolidate your loans once. So if interest rates decrease, you cannot simply reconsolidate. The only exception is if you have gone back to school and acquired another student loan. Then you can consolidate to join your new loan with your old one.

7. It's always a good idea to check with a financial advisor before consolidating. The information in this book is a guideline, but each person's situation is very specific. Good advice can save you thousands, so always be open to a professional opinion.

Now let's get going. The most vital part of this process is going to be your mindset. Set your mind on the right path, and everything will follow.

"Progress is impossible without change, and those who cannot change their minds cannot change anything." - George Bernard Shaw

5 THE MENTALITY

There are two paths when it comes to student loans, the most common is what I call the "path to coping." I've seen this in most of my friends. They graduate with a Religious Studies degree and $100,000 in student loan debt. What university thought it was a good idea to allow a student to accrue $100,000 in loans to obtain a degree which, according to Forbes, has one of the highest unemployment rates, and on average pays no greater than $30,000 per year? Another friend of mine has over $120,000 in school debt with a Fine Arts degree. Others have higher paying degrees such as Law, but are finding the workforce swarming with out-of-work lawyers. Meanwhile, they have a staggering $160,000 in student loan debt. While most of my friends have about $20-$40,000 in student loan debt, the mentality is the same. They give up. Student loans become an unavoidable part of life.

In some ways it becomes a good war story. I found myself sitting around with friends talking about how screwed up we were financially and who could top who. This somewhat depressing competition becomes the norm because we just want to be comfortable with where we are. It's the tribe mentality. We all belong to the generation of debtors. Thinking of our debt as a normal consequence of education makes it more palatable. So the tribe accepts you, and we all feel ok because we can sit together in the mud. If we accept debt as a part of life, we don't have to change anything, especially ourselves. Dave Ramsey is a financial adviser and talk show host whom I highly recommend. In Dave's book, *Total Money Makeover*, he says it like this: "Change is painful. Few people have the courage to seek out change. Most people won't change until the pain of where they are exceeds the pain of change. When it comes to money, we can be like the toddler in a soiled diaper. 'I know it smells bad, but it's warm and it's mine'" (15).

It's time to take the diaper off . . . um, in a philosophical sort of way. This means that we stop accepting debt as a part of life. It is sold to us as essential, but the very idea of debt is a cycle of death. To establish good credit, you need to go into debt. Once you're in debt and begin to pay it back slowly over time, you establish good credit so you can go further into debt. Sounds pretty dumb. So let's stop thinking that debt is ok; let's decide that it is a slaveholder who tells you what to do on a daily basis. Take your life back, say no to debt - both current and future.

It is essential to understand that this change happens within. There are no quick repayment systems; no one wants to give you their money so you can pay off your student loans. The government isn't going to help you. The only way to change your current situation is to decide deep within yourself that you will fight for the freedom of your finances and refuse to be a slave to the lender. You can. You will. End of story.

This brings us to the other path, what I call the "path to freedom." This path says *I am the master of my fate*. Debt is *not* ok. On this path we refuse to accept debt as our master and decide we're going to be financially free. The importance of this mindset cannot be overstated. Do not accept the lie that school debt is "good" debt, and should be paid off on a standard payment plan to build credit. Recognize that debt is a parasite. It drains the life from you, and it needs to die.

So how do you apply this mental shift? The best tool you can utilize is this: every time you see something you want, ask yourself, "Do I need this to survive?" I'm not talking about simple *need* versus *want* because this can get a little confusing. Especially when you see something you've always wanted, and it's on sale! So you need to ask yourself, "Do I need this to *survive*?" If the answer is yes, buy it, if the answer is no, don't. I mean this quite literally. If there is any way you can go on living without making this purchase, don't buy it.

A good friend of mine, Johnathan, used to come to work each day with an old cereal box. I thought he loved cereal until I realized he was using it to carry his lunch. After a good laugh, I asked him why he didn't buy a new lunch box. His response floored me, "because I don't need one." Johnathan was already living this mindset. He knew that he could survive without a new lunch box, so he used what he had. Six months later he was still using a cardboard box to pack his lunch. People thought he was crazy, but he knew what he was doing. Johnathan applied this question to everything in his life. One day people were rolling their eyes at his makeshift lunch box, and the next day, he and his wife departed on a six-month trek through Europe. No one ever commented on Johnathan's lunch box again.

If you use this mindset for every purchase, you're setting yourself up for success as you begin your journey to pay back your student loans. Once your student loans are paid off, you can buy yourself a new lunch box, or keep using your cereal box and see where the world takes you.

The second tool that you need to utilize is: if you don't have the money to buy it outright, then don't get it! Save until you can afford the item. This means no payment plans or rent-to-own. We will cover these topics in greater detail later.

Your mental shift is the foundation that everything else will build upon. You have taken your first step down the path to freedom. Now let's get to the tough stuff: how do we accelerate your debt payments? How do you double or even triple your monthly payments and pay off your school debt in 3 to 4 years instead of 10 to 30? It all starts with a simple budget.

"The budget is not just a collection of numbers, but an expression of our values and aspirations." - Jacob Lew

6 THE BUDGET

Most people see their monthly income as a bowl full of possibility. When their paycheck is deposited in their account, they look to that money and live life accordingly. If they see something they want, and have the money in their account, they buy it. When you look at the money first, and spend according to what you think you have, you usually run out of money long before all the bills are paid and begin living paycheck to paycheck. As soon as more money enters the account, it's a huge relief and the spending begins again. Bills begin to be paid late, credit cards start holding balances longer than a month, and debt grows. Even if you make enough money to keep paying your bills, you never really know where all the money is going each month.

Have you ever put a bunch of cash in your wallet and a few days later realized most of it was gone, but you had no idea where it went? This is very common, and why people say money burns a hole in your pocket. It just seems to disappear. Or maybe at the end of the month you check your credit card balance and are shocked by the massive bill and have no idea how you racked up that much debt? When this happened I would get mad and wish I knew where it went. I felt out of control, like someone stole that money from my pocket, or I lost it. I finally realized a powerful truth. If you don't control your finances and spending, it will control you. Once you run out of money, you have no control left; you're now at the mercy of your credit lenders. So control your own money; know where it comes from and where it goes every month. Rather than looking at the money first, we are going to turn this around, and look at how much it costs for you to live, eat, and pay your bills on a monthly basis. Here comes the budget.

Many people see a budget as a restriction. They don't want to be bound by financial rules they have to follow. They want to be "in control" of where their money goes each month, not be bound by some rules as to how they can spend their hard earned dollar. But in reality, if you don't know where your money is going, you're not in control after all. A budget doesn't control you; it allows you to control your money and therefore your life.

By listing out all of your expenses for each month, you're able to plan where your money will go. You have to eat, so you set aside money for food. You have to pay for a place to live, so you set aside rent or mortgage money. What about your car insurance? Well, that is paid at the end of the year, so you don't have to worry about that one. Actually, yes you do. As a matter of fact that is the perfect example of a good budget. Everyone dreads the moment an annual bill arrives because all of a sudden you owe a huge chunk of money that you don't have. You scrape and claw enough money together to pay the bill or maybe put it on a credit card and pay 18% interest until you pay it off. Instead, imagine when the $900 car insurance bill arrives, that you open an envelope and there is $900 in cash ready to pay your bill. Or when the car breaks down, and you need to pay $400 for a new timing belt, you open an envelope and there is $400 in cash waiting to pay for your car. Wouldn't it be nice if you didn't have to worry about how your bills will be paid? You want to go out to a nice restaurant but you don't know if you can afford it, so you look in your "fun money" envelope and see $200 set aside just for you. Without fear or guilt, you pull the money out and go have a great time.

A budget shouldn't restrict you. It should free you to spend your money as you wish, and have confidence that you can pay all of your bills through the entire year. There are a lot of ways to budget. Some banks have virtual wallets where you can create different categories and have money deposited in each category. There are free websites like Mint.com that help you organize your spending. When I counsel people, I recommend the cash envelope system. It has been used for over a hundred years and is a great way to physically see your available money and control your finances. All you need for an envelope system is a box or organizer and a bunch of envelopes. You write an expense category on each of the envelopes and mark the amount of money you're setting aside. At the end or beginning of the month you withdraw cash from your bank account and fill the envelopes according to how much you think you will spend in each of the expense categories.

Here is a list of common budget categories:
- Baby – Diapers, etc.
- Cable/Internet
- Car Insurance
- Car Maintenance
- Car Payment
- Cell Phone
- Christmas
- Clothing
- Food
- Fun Money/Entertainment
- Gas – for vehicle
- Gifts
- House Maintenance
- Life Insurance
- Medical Expenses
- Memberships
- Personal/Home products – cleaning, bathroom, etc.
- Rent or Mortgage
- Tithe
- Travel
- Utilities

You won't need all of these envelopes, so pick the ones that apply to you. Decide how much you will spend, and fill your envelopes. For example, you can put $350 in a food envelope. When it's time to go shopping, use the cash. When the money is gone, you stop shopping. Some people don't like carrying cash on them. If you're not comfortable keeping cash, I recommend using a debit card for your purchases. When you get home, take the equivalent amount of money from your food envelope and deposit it back in your bank account. You may wonder: why don't you just leave the money in your account and keep track on paper? You can do that if you're meticulous at keeping track, bringing home every receipt, and never missing a purchase. Most people don't want to spend that much energy on their budget, so an envelope system is best. If you need to buy food, you go to the envelope and take out the cash; it's easy to know when you have spent all of your food money . . . the envelope is empty. Then you eat out of your freezer until the end of the month when you refill your budget envelopes.

The envelope system is very clean, precise, and avoids many numerical errors or a lack of receipt tracking. Personally, I like to keep an Excel spreadsheet of my spending. I still use the envelope system, but every time I purchase something or make a payment, I log it in a spreadsheet. Over the years, I can look back and see where I am spending my money and make changes. Not everyone will keep up with a spreadsheet, so feel free to start with cash envelopes. If you have money left over at the end of the month, leave it in the envelope. You may need it the next month. If you consistently have money left over, think about reducing how much you put in the envelope. Most likely you will find you're overspending and do not have enough in a certain envelope. Perhaps you need to curb your spending, or you may need to increase how much you allot to that category. A budget won't work perfectly right away. There will be growing pains for the first few months as you run out of money in some areas and don't spend all of it in others. That's ok; keep adjusting the budget until you're staying within the limits you have placed. It will probably take three to five months before the budget is working consistently.

The last aspect of a budget is the emergency fund. I recommend building up $1,000 in your emergency fund in case you have a financial emergency. This prevents the "credit card cycle." The credit card cycle is when you have an unexpected bill and no money to pay it. You don't have the money, so you put the bill on a credit card. The next month you begin paying on the credit card and the moment you pay it off another unexpected bill shows up in the mail. This cycle is really discouraging and can kill your motivation to pay off your debt. It feels like you're always playing catch up and never in control. When you have $1,000 in your emergency fund, you can pay that bill with cash. Then build that emergency fund back up to $1,000 before paying down your debt. When another emergency strikes, you're ready. Having a small emergency fund will buffer unknown expenses and give you more control when things don't go as planned. It also keeps you motivated because you're always in the positive, rather than feeling like you're always living in the negative.

If you're still feeling like a budget isn't worth it, or feeling trapped by the idea, just try it! It took a long time before I was convinced to do it, but I've felt so much freedom with my money since I started budgeting. I don't have to worry about money at all because my budget sets aside what I need to live. Money doesn't stress me out anymore. There is no fear or anxiety over losing money because I know exactly where it goes each month. There isn't any guilt over buying something for myself because that money is set-aside in my "fun money" envelope. It is so liberating! I encourage you to take some time to write up a preliminary budget so you can reference it as we go through the rest of the book.

A budget will help you get control of your finances, but the real secret to paying down your student loan is free money.

"The lack of money is the root of all evil." - Mark Twain

7 FREE MONEY

As a kid, my favorite book was *Peter and the Penny Tree* by Thomas James. The story was about a boy named Peter and a tree that kept growing pennies. Back then you could still buy a tootsie roll or a Swedish fish for a penny so imagine how delighted I was at the thought of a tree full of pennies that could buy me unlimited candy. So I went home and planted a penny in the dirt outside our city apartment. Every day I went outside and scanned the dirt looking for anything growing. Aside from a few weeds, nothing grew in that hard city dirt. Soon I realized that no amount of sun or water could get my penny tree to grow, and my disappointed 5-year-old self became disillusioned. As I scrounged the dirt for my wasted penny I saw a glint of copper shining up at me. It was a penny, but not the one I had buried. My mother's boyfriend later recognized I had found an Indian Head penny and offered me a dollar. My penny tree was a failure, but I didn't care; I had a dollar! I learned a valuable lesson that day: money doesn't grow on trees, but you can find free money if you're willing to get your hands dirty.

You're probably not going to pay off your student loans by finding pennies in the dirt. So we need to dig deeper to find some substantial money for you.

Let's take a quick look at an income breakdown for a post-graduate in the workforce making $40,000 per year. This is by no means exhaustive, but rather a general look at the common expenses and taxes we have to pay.

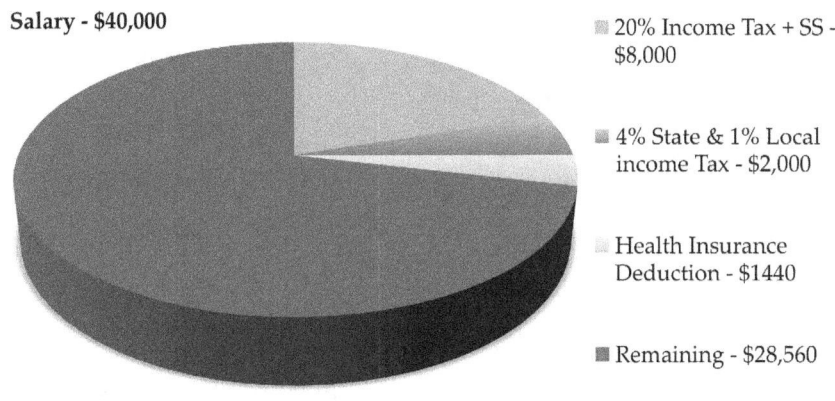

Salary - $40,000

- 20% Income Tax + SS - $8,000
- 4% State & 1% Local income Tax - $2,000
- Health Insurance Deduction - $1440
- Remaining - $28,560

After Income tax- Federal, State, Local, and Social Security-the postgraduate is making $30,000. Subtract health insurance and the total net income is $28,560. Broken down to monthly income, we have $2,380 to work with each month. Now let's break things down further and define where the monthly income will be spent in a postgraduate budget.

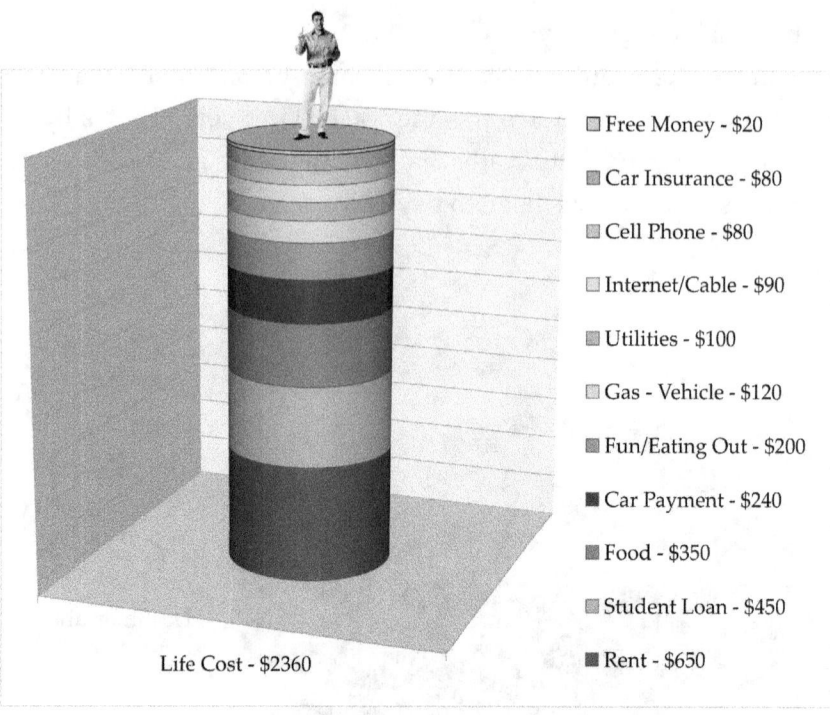

Free Money - $20
Car Insurance - $80
Cell Phone - $80
Internet/Cable - $90
Utilities - $100
Gas - Vehicle - $120
Fun/Eating Out - $200
Car Payment - $240
Food - $350
Student Loan - $450
Rent - $650

Life Cost - $2360

Even though we all have different levels of income, debt, expenses, and challenges, we are going to assume the postgraduate above is you. The different budgeted items are defined on the right with the amount of money they take from your life. We are going to call this your "life cost." Your life cost is simply how much money it takes for you to live, eat, and pay your required bills. A lot of people have no idea how much money they spend every month on their life cost. In fact they often spend *more* money than they *make*.

Bill Earle is attributed with saying, "If your outgo exceeds your income, then your upkeep will be your downfall." It's pretty simple; if you spend more than you make, you're in trouble. Take the United States government, for example. The U.S. received $3.2 trillion in 2016, but they spent $3.8 trillion. This left a $600 billion budget deficit. Every year the government spends more than it makes which is why the U.S. now owes 20 trillion dollars. But if you spend less than you make you'll have money left over, which is the ultimate goal.

Let's get back to your budget. You make $2,380 per month, and you're standing on $2,360 per month in expenses. You have $20 in money left over each month. Do you see that thin sliver on top? Yup, that's all you have left, and $20 is not a lot of money to make a financial change in your life. So how do you free up more money?

When you look at this pillar, you see the majority of your money going towards life expenses. Imagine if you could shift these sections and reduce your rent, food, car costs, insurance, utilities, and cell phone bill. By decreasing your life cost, you're giving your money a get-out-of-jail-free card, and no one can hold it anymore except for you. No one is requiring you to put that money towards any bills, debt collectors, or expenses. It is not bound to anyone or anything. Sounds pretty "free," right? Exactly, this is what we are going to call, "free money." Money that you can use to buy whatever you want or ideally, pay down your student loan debt. It's time to unshackle your finances, so you can reduce your life cost as much as possible and create free money. Free money is where you create the power for real, impactful change. Without free money, you're limited to making your minimum student loan payment for the longest duration allowed. The terrible truth is, the longer it takes to pay off your student loans, the more interest you pay, extending your debt instead of obliterating it.

"Albert Einstein when asked what he considered to be the most powerful force in the universe answered: Compound interest! . . ."
- Mignon McLaughlin

8 INTEREST AND PAYMENTS

Every month your student loan accrues interest. If you're $65,000 in debt at an interest rate of 7%, you will accrue around $400 per month in interest. That means if you didn't pay your student loans ,because you were in forbearance, the loans would *increase* by $400 per month. Compounding interest means interest is charged on the principal amount, the $65,000, plus the interest that is accrued, which is the $400 per month. So after one month you will owe $65,400. After the second month you will owe 7% interest on the total amount of $65,400, so you will now owe $65,803. The additional $3 in this last example doesn't look like much. So let's look at the difference between regular and compounding interest if you didn't make any payments on your student loans over 12 years. If the interest *was not* compounding, you would accrue $54,600 in interest. If the interest *was* compounding monthly, you would accrue $85,196 in interest. That's a difference of over $30,000! That is the power of compounding interest. The longer you have your loan, the more interest is charged on your principal amount and the interest it accrues. Scary, right? That is why you have to pay off your debt as fast as possible.

With your loans being $65,000, you should be paying $700 a month for about 12 years. But your life cost in chapter 7 shows you only have about $450 to put towards your loans. Well that's a simple fix, right? You can just reduce your monthly payment. So you reduce the payment to $450 per month for 30 years. Sure, you're paying for a longer period of time but you're also paying less per month, so it's basically the same, right? Let's see just how well that works out for you.

Month	Payment	Interest	Principal	$65,000
1	$450	$400	$50	$64,950
2	$450	$400	$50	$64,900
3	$450	$400	$50	$64,850
4	$450	$400	$50	$64,800
5	$450	$400	$50	$64,750
6	$450	$400	$50	$64,700
7	$450	$400	$50	$64,650
8	$450	$400	$50	$64,600
9	$450	$400	$50	$64,550
10	$450	$400	$50	$64,500
11	$450	$400	$50	$64,450
12	$450	$400	$50	$64,400

When you make a payment of $450, the first $400 is taken to pay for interest. That means the remaining $50 goes towards the principal. Even though you're paying them $450 per month, you're only reducing your debt each month by $50! In twelve months, you have paid $5,400 in student loan payments and only reduced your student loan by $600. After two years of paying your student loans, you will have paid them $10,800 but only reduced your student loans by $1,200. That seems ridiculous, but a lot of people are making minimum payments or paying interest only.

Let's think of it this way: the interest that is accrued each month on your student loan is like a wall. It is stopping you from reaching your debt and paying it down. In order to reach your principal debt, you have to climb this wall every month. So you pile up $400 in front of the wall, so you can now reach your debt. If you have $50 left over, you can reduce your debt by that same amount. Every month you set $400 against that wall and climb up. But what happens if this time you have $950 to put against your loan? When you pile the $400 against the wall, you can take the other $550 and put it directly against your principal. You have to pile that $400 against the wall every month no matter what. That part doesn't change. What can change is the amount you put against your loans on top of the $400 interest wall payment.

The more you pay down the principal, the lower your interest charge per month. This means the wall gets shorter and shorter. Once you reduce your principal to 32,500, you're only charged $200 per month in interest. The wall is now half the size, and that means it takes less to climb your interest wall. So now you have more money left over to pay down your principal and your payment is more powerful. Every time you make a payment over the interest wall, you lower the principal loan balance, and that is the ultimate goal.

According to your life cost above, you only have $20 in free money per month. Now imagine that every month you're given an additional $500. All of your bills in your life cost are already paid, so this money is free and clear of any responsibility. It is truly free money. You can put the $500 directly towards your student loans. Let's redo the math. If you can put $450 towards your student loans, only $50 goes towards the principal. If you can put $950 against your student loans each month, $550 goes towards the principal.

Month	Payment	Interest	Principal	$65,000
1	$950	$400	$550	$64,450
2	$950	$400	$550	$63,900
3	$950	$400	$550	$63,350
4	$950	$400	$550	$62,800
5	$950	$400	$550	$62,250
6	$950	$400	$550	$61,700
7	$950	$400	$550	$61,150
8	$950	$400	$550	$60,600
9	$950	$400	$550	$60,050
10	$950	$400	$550	$59,500
11	$950	$400	$550	$58,950
12	$950	$400	$550	$58,400

If we compare the two payment schedules, this is what we see over a 12 month period:

Scenario 1 - $450 per month for 12 months:

Payment Total	Interest	Principal Paid	Debt Total
$5,400	$4,800	$600	$64,400

Scenario 2- $950 per month for 12 months:

Payment Total	Interest	Principal Paid	Debt Total
$11,400	$4,800	$6,600	$58,400

By paying $950 per month, you paid a total of $11,400 in one year- a little more than double what you paid in the first scenario. In the first scenario, you only reduced your student loan by $600. But in the second, you have reduced your student loan principal by $6,600. **You paid a little more than double your first payment, but paid off more than ten times the principal amount!** You have climbed the interest wall and are putting the money where it matters: against the principal loan. After two years, Scenario 1 will have paid them $10,800 and reduced the principal by $1,200; Scenario 2 paid $22,800, and reduced your student loans by $13,200. Again, you're paying a little more than double the payment, but paying down over ten times the principal.

Obviously you want to increase the principal payment as much as possible. Every dollar you free up becomes another dollar of free money that goes directly to reducing your student loan principal. You have climbed the interest wall, and you're making a difference where it matters. But who is going to give you $500 per month? The answer is simple: *you are.*

Think of it like this. A man decides to go on a boat ride in the ocean. He takes along his cell phone, TV, computer, magazine collection, baseball cards, an X-box, and a PlayStation. After sailing a few days into the ocean, he notices that some of the magazines are getting wet. He looks down to find there is a hole in the side of the boat. This hole is letting water into the boat, and unless he starts bailing, it will slowly sink him. The hole is his student loan payment, and the water is the interest. So he begins bailing water. Every day, a certain amount of water leaks into the boat. If the man times everything correctly, he can still play his X-box and PlayStation, and still use his TV and cell phone while just keeping up with bailing the water out. There is never a thought to patching the hole because it takes all of his effort to bail out the water each day. In 20 to 30 years, he will reach the shore, and this watery mess will all be over. But one day he realizes, if he cuts out one thing, say his cell phone, he will have more energy to focus on the hole in his boat. So he throws his cell phone out. Now he has some energy to begin looking for patching material. Then he keeps going, by setting aside his X-box and PlayStation. Now he's not just barely staying afloat, he's making progress. He is finding he has twice or three times as much energy to deal with this leaking boat. Taking his magazines and baseball cards, he fashions a plug that stops the boat from leaking. With the boat fixed, he can sail away without fear of sinking.

Let's do the same with your life cost. Let's decrease your life cost and increase your free money so you can apply it to the principal debt. Now you just need the tools. Remember the penny tree? It may take some digging, but we can find free money for you. It's time to get your hands dirty.

"Money equals freedom." - Kevin O'Leary

9 THE POWER OF "PER-MONTH"

The first way to get free money is to learn to avoid the traps laid by marketing companies and businesses. Let's look at "per-month payment plans." Most people see things they want, so they purchase them. Or more commonly, they are shopping for a $900 laptop and see the little sign that says, "Only $30 per month!" Usually, a zero percent interest sign follows. You're getting a $900 laptop for $30 per month with no interest. How you can you beat that? The better question is, how are they benefiting from letting you use their money to buy something? The two strategies employed by companies are: selling the laptop for more than it's worth but in smaller increments, and secondly, expecting people to miss a payment and charging them really high interest as a result.

The first strategy is to sell the item for more than its value. You see a laptop being sold by the manufacturer for $900, but you don't have the money. Instead, you find another website that will sell it to you for $30 a month for 4 years with no interest. Seems like a good deal until you do the math, and please know that most people never do the math. They assume the company is selling the laptop for a similar price. But $30 a month for 4 years is $1,440. By the time you finish paying off the laptop, you have paid $540 more than you should.

The second strategy is selling the laptop for the same price but anticipating a missed payment. In this scenario, the laptop is being sold for $30 a month for 3 years, which equals $900 with zero interest for 3 years. Sounds perfect, except in the fine print it states that if you miss a single payment, they can charge you the full interest for all three years immediately. The interest rate in the fine print is 29%. So the first time you miss a payment, or a mistake happens with your form of payment, you're charged 29% on the spot. That would be a hefty $261 per year in interest. Since they can immediately charge you all of the interest for the full 3 years, you now owe an additional $783. You have almost doubled the cost of your laptop. Statistically, the majority of people miss a payment, and it doesn't matter if you miss your first or last payment, the full interest will be charged immediately.

Per-month expenses are the primary killer of free money. Avoid them like the plague. Some things like cell phones and internet can't be avoided, but make sure to get the absolute lowest rate.

"Poor people are those who only work to try to keep an expensive lifestyle and always want more and more." - Jose Mujica

10 INCREASING YOUR FREE MONEY:

HOUSING AND UTILITIES

When I first graduated college, I wanted to move into an apartment by myself. I had endured roommates all through college and was done dealing with other people. Working hard for my money meant I deserved to have my own space. Then I started looking for apartments and realized a one bedroom in my area would cost at least $650. The cost of utilities would be entirely mine, and winters here can be cold. I looked at my life cost and decided that roommates could save me a lot of money. At the time, I had no idea how much.

A one bedroom was $650, a two bedroom was $800. Splitting a two bedroom with one roommate would reduce my rent from $650 to $400. A three to four bedroom house rented for $1,000 a month. The most I could save would be with four guys in one house with a monthly rent of $250 per month. So that's what I did. Three of my friends and I moved into a very nice house. Of course they didn't clean as much as I would have liked, didn't mow the lawn like we agreed, and once we even put caution tape around the mountain of trash in the kitchen that one roommate just refused to remove. It wasn't easy, but it was worth it, because I not only saved rent but also utilities and added expenses.

Our heat and electricity was split between the four of us. This greatly reduced my monthly life cost. Rather than paying $100 per month for electric in a one bedroom, I only paid $35 per month. Whereas internet and cable would have been $90 by myself, it was only $10 split between the four of us. We decided not to have cable TV, which is a choice I always recommend. I'll talk more about that later. If I had lived alone, I would have paid $650 in rent, $100 in electricity, and $90 in cable/internet, which totals $840 per month. By living with roommates, my costs decreased to $250 in rent, $35 in electricity, and $10 for internet. My living expenses dropped from $840 to $295 per month. *That means I created $545 of free money per month by changing my living situation.*

Some people will refuse to do this because they "deserve" to live alone, or they simply don't want to make the sacrifice. I can't blame them. Living with other people is hard, but rewarding. The friendships you develop can last a lifetime and the savings cannot be matched. This is the biggest way to create free money for yourself. And remember, this isn't forever; it is only while you pay off your student loans. The few years you have after college are the perfect time to hit them hard and get them paid off. So if you refuse to consider this, please stop and really think about what this could mean. My $545 of free money each month meant that every year I was paying an additional $6,540 against my student loans. Over four years alone I made an additional $26,160 worth of student loan payments because of my living situation.

Not everyone is single when they come out of college or when they pick up this book. If you're married or own your home, this can still apply to you. My wife and I bought our first house and immediately invited a friend to rent a spare room. The extra monthly income helped tremendously towards paying off our mortgage. If you have two spare rooms, rent them both. Through our ten years of marriage we have spent most of them living in community with other people. It wasn't easy or convenient, but it allowed us to pay off our first house in less than four years and continue to buy more rental properties. This style of living works, and it has powerful returns.

Perhaps living in community with others will not work for you. There is a movement of minimalists who are dedicated to getting rid of excess in their lives. This excess includes big houses. Houses in the United States are over twice the size that they were 30 years ago, despite the fact that the average household has half the amount of children. These minimalists have chosen to go in the opposite direction, and live in tiny houses. When I say tiny houses, I mean *really* tiny. Some of the houses are only 100 square feet. Imagine how cheap it would be to heat a house that is only 10ft x 10ft? It's a growing movement that is popping up all over the internet.

My wife and I experimented with this style of living for almost a year. Our tiny home was about 200 square feet. We had a master bedroom, a tiny bunk room for our 2-year-old son, and a kitchen/living room area. It was tight, but we made that space our home, and it didn't take long before it was a normal life for us. You would be surprised what you can get used to if you're willing to try. Our rent was pretty much nothing and the utility bills were dirt cheap. The best part was how easy it was to keep the space clean because, well there wasn't much space. It was a fun adventure, and one we hope to return to after our kids are older. You may not have the option of living in a tiny house community, but get used to the idea of living in a *really* small apartment. Get the cheapest, smallest apartment that you're comfortable with. The rent will be lower, and it will be a lot cheaper to heat and cool your living space.

If you really want to supercharge your savings, look for a part time job that offers free housing, such as a property attendant.

Apartment buildings and condos need someone to be on property full time. The job requires you to do office work, receive calls, and do showings, in exchange for a salary and free housing. Another option is a residential assistant for students or special needs clients. They usually need someone to sleep through the night, so they offer free housing, utilities, and sometimes food.

The final option has a bad reputation. Most of us know at least one person in their mid-twenties, or even thirties, still living in their parent's basement. Some of you will cringe at the thought. Others may not think it's a big deal at all. Setting any stigma aside, this is by far the cheapest living situation you can find. Some parents may ask you to contribute to the bills, but others will offer free housing, utilities, and even food. If you really want to annihilate your student loans, stop to consider the drastic change this would make in your finances.

For most of you, this will not be an option. So for the sake of our calculations, we won't assume this is the path you will take. Instead, we will continue by reducing housing costs from living in a one bedroom alone to living with roommates.

So if we apply this principle to the life cost listed above, you reduce rent from $650 to $250 per month. But you also reduce utilities from $100 to $35 per month, and by cutting the cable and only paying for internet, you reduce that cost to $10 per month. Let's apply that to your life cost pillar and see how much free money you're able to create.

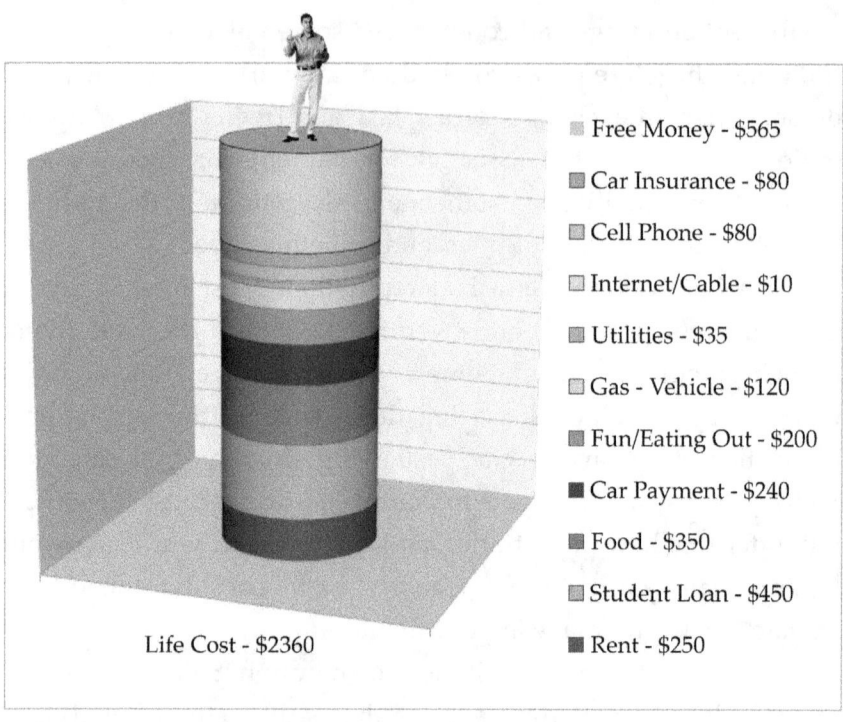

Life Cost - $2360

- Free Money - $565
- Car Insurance - $80
- Cell Phone - $80
- Internet/Cable - $10
- Utilities - $35
- Gas - Vehicle - $120
- Fun/Eating Out - $200
- Car Payment - $240
- Food - $350
- Student Loan - $450
- Rent - $250

Take a look at the free money available. You went from $20 to $565 per month. This money is free and clear of any and all responsibility. Which means you could spend it however you like- aka put it against your student loans. If you did, you would reduce your student loan principal by $6,780 in one year.

You can focus on today and think, "It's only a few hundred dollars more to live alone," or you can think about tomorrow and decide, "If I sacrifice now, I can pay an additional $26,160 against my student loans in just four years." You can. You will. End of story.

"I can't change the direction of the wind, but I can adjust my sails to always reach my destination." - Jimmy Dean

VEHICLES

Cars are expensive. This is going to be a bit crazy but hear me out. If you don't need a car . . . don't get one. Most people can't imagine living without a car, but public transportation is a viable option. You not only save on a car payment, but you save on repairs, gas, and car insurance. The total money saved by not owning a car is staggering. Imagine saving $240 a month for the car payment, $50 per month in maintenance, $100 per month in gas, and $80 per month for car insurance. Your savings would be $470 a month. That's $5,640 per year in life cost savings and, you guessed it, $5,640 of free money. Over four years, it totals $22,560. You're probably seeing the trend here. In fact, only 9% of the world's population even has a car. So join the trendy, or be a trendsetter, and tell your friends by not having a car, someone is paying you $5,000 per year. (You will need the $640 for bus and train fare.)

For most people, this isn't practical, or they are not willing to make the sacrifice, and again I understand. When I graduated college, I did buy a car. But never buy a new car; it loses a third of its value the minute it rolls off the sales lot. Contrary to what people think, vehicles are not an investment; they are a liability. Meaning they take money from you. Unless your part time job is driving for Uber; cars rarely make you money.

My recommendation is to look for an older car with low mileage and preferably from a little old lady who kept it in her garage. I've purchased 3 vehicles in my time, and they were all old cars with low miles purchased from little old ladies. I'm not kidding. They were usually a Honda or Toyota because the engines run forever. Go online and research which cars rate the highest in reliability. Then set your sights on those cars and scour the internet and local newspapers. My first car was a Geo Prizm, which has a Toyota engine. I purchased it for $1,200 cash and drove it for over 100,000 miles. It lasted me ten years and saved me a ton of money in car payments. My car also got 40 miles per gallon, so the gas savings were huge. In the course of these ten years, there were some things I had to sacrifice. The AC didn't work, neither did the interior dome light. A few of the interior door handles broke, and the rear window was broken out by a random thrown rock, (which I repaired with a piece of plexy glass.) The radio stopped working, as well as the heat, and the fabric interior was stapled up because it kept ripping and falling down. The fan and blower shorted out one day, but the car still ran. I had no windshield wiper fluid because the tank was missing, the front end was poorly repaired from a fender bender, and the hood was crumpled. When people saw my car, they pitied me and encouraged me to submit it to the show *Pimp My Ride* because it was that bad. (I tried, but they only accept submissions from people in California.) The car was pathetic, but even after all of these things, I still ran that car for another four years. Why did I do it? I did it because I didn't *need* another car. Did I *want* another car? Absolutely! But I didn't *need* another car, so I kept driving it- waiting for it to die. Finally, when it wouldn't pass inspection without investing a lot of money, I sold the car to a recycling center for $300. So what was my car payment if I bought the car for $1,200, drove it for 10 years, and sold it for $300? My monthly car payment was $7.50 per month. Not everyone will get a car that doesn't quit. But many people buy newer cars because they are tired of their old car, or simply feel it's unreliable or too old. They use a "today" mentality. They decide a few hundred dollars per month isn't that expensive, instead of looking at their life cost, and deciding to get free money for their tomorrow. If you're working to increase your free money, don't buy another car! Keep driving your old car.

Sometimes when you drive an older car, they need more maintenance. Set aside maintenance money in your budget so you have it when you need it. Even if you save $100 a month in an envelope for maintenance, it's still a lot lower than a car payment, and your insurance premium will be a lot lower on an old car. You want to buy an inexpensive older car, with a reliable reputation, and with lower miles. There are a lot of them out there for $1,000 to $2,000. It may not look great, but if it gets you where you need to go, that's all that matters.

I also never recommend a lease. The payment is slightly lower, but all of the maintenance costs are still yours, and at the end of the lease, you have nothing to show for it. They limit your miles and charge you extra fees if you exceed them. Leases are always a bad idea.

So let's apply your new car cost to your life cost pillar. First, you avoid a car payment or a lease, and buy an older used car that gets good gas mileage. Every month, you avoid the $240 car payment. You're also going to reduce your gas because you're more concerned with getting a car that gets 33-40 miles per gallon than getting a convertible. So now you reduce your gas from $120 per month to $80 per month. The other savings come from car insurance. If you bought your car with cash, there is no bank loan requiring you to carry collision. If the car is only worth a few thousand dollars, it's usually better to just have liability and comprehensive coverage on your car. Collision is best if the car has a lot of value. If you're not comfortable dropping collision on an older, cheap car, I understand; but it's probably not worth the coverage. So now you have reduced your car insurance payment from $80 per month to $55 per month. That's another $25 per month. Your total car savings include: car payment $240, gas savings $40, and insurance reduction $25, which totals $305 per month. You still have a car to drive; it's just not brand new or fancy, but it's economical and the pathway to financial freedom. Before we total your life pillar, let's put $100 of that money back into a car maintenance fund. Even if we set aside $100 for a car maintenance fund, you have still increased your free money by $205 per month. That's $2,460 per year and $9,840 in four years. Your life cost pillar now has $770 per month in free money.

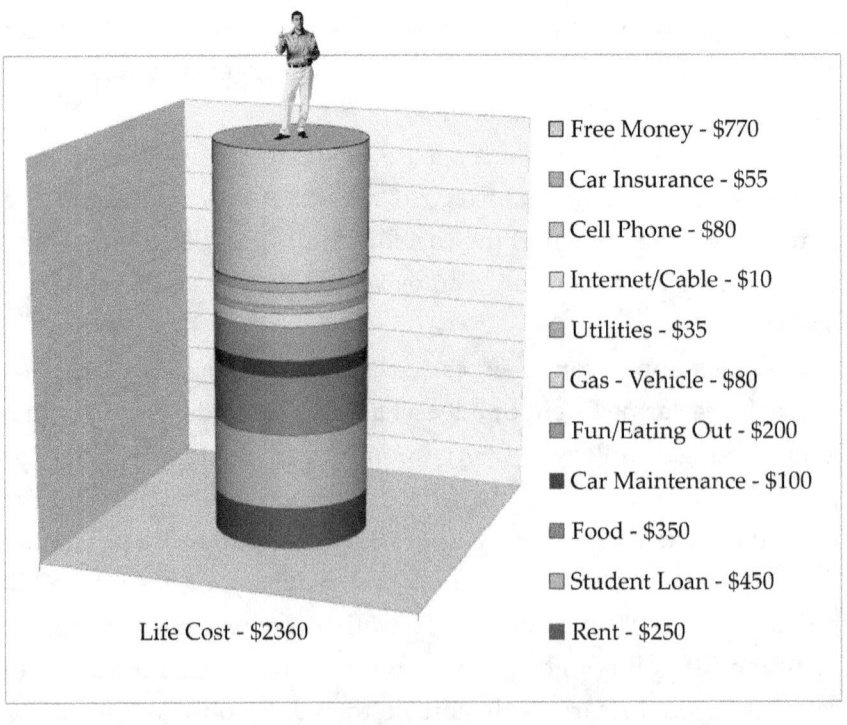

Life Cost - $2360

- Free Money - $770
- Car Insurance - $55
- Cell Phone - $80
- Internet/Cable - $10
- Utilities - $35
- Gas - Vehicle - $80
- Fun/Eating Out - $200
- Car Maintenance - $100
- Food - $350
- Student Loan - $450
- Rent - $250

"A man in debt is so far a slave." - Ralph Waldo Emerson

CELL PHONES, INTERNET, CABLE & OTHER PER-MONTH EXPENSES

Remember, for every dollar you don't spend on your life cost you have increased a dollar in your free money. That money is clear of any responsibility for that month, so you can apply it directly to your principal debt. Common per-month charges include cell phone, internet, and cable. When you look at a cell phone bill, you may see three options: a basic phone plan for $40 per month, a nicer plan for $60, or the premier plan for $80 per month. It's only a $40 difference between the $40 plan and the $80 plan, right? Let's also consider a difference of $3.50 in taxes on whichever plan you choose. Sounds stupid to be thinking about $3.50 in taxes, but believe me, it's not. So what does the $43.50 difference really mean to you? Over the course of one year, it's $522. Let's assume you're on a ten-year payment plan for your student loans. Over the full ten years, you have lost $5,220. You have actually lost more than $5,220, but we will cover how compounding interest affects your expenses later.

If you need to have a smart phone with unlimited data, make sure you shop around. Don't assume the big companies are the only ones with reliable service. There are many smaller cell providers that use the major companies' cell towers. The service coverage is still excellent, but the price is considerably cheaper. As of 2017, Cricket, who is owned by AT&T and uses their towers, has cell plans with unlimited talk, text, and internet for $35 per month after taxes. Republic wireless uses Sprint towers and has an "unlimited everything" plan for $25 per month or unlimited talk and text for $10 per month. Shop around for every purchase you make, especially if it's a per-month commitment. Remember, per-month expenses kill your free money.

We've already cut the cable bill in your scenario and reduced the internet to $10 per month because you've chosen to live with other people and share the expense. That was a good choice because with Netflix, Hulu, and Amazon Prime, most of my friends do not even have cable TV. They get a great internet promotion and utilize the internet for all of their TV viewing needs. My wife and I have not owned a TV for the past ten years. We spend our time reading, writing, or pursuing other dreams that bring us financial freedom. If we want to watch something, we use our laptop. The freedom of not having a TV playing all the time in the living room encourages conversation and real interaction with each other and friends. This may be a bit radical for some, so take steps as you see fit. Just make sure you first ask yourself, "Do I *need* this to survive, or do I just *want* this?" If you need internet, which most of us do, then get it. Unless you need cable TV, avoid it and save the money. The extra $30 to $80 a month will add up to thousands of dollars in a very short time.

Per-month purchasing is about getting what you want right now and not worrying about how it will affect you in the future. It's so easy to think that $20 a month isn't a lot of money, but it is, because every $20 adds up to hundreds of dollars a year and thousands of dollars over the course of a few years. Stop thinking about today, and start thinking about your tomorrow. It's the only way to obtain financial freedom.

The per-month strategy is really the same as rent-to-own, so avoid that like the plague. If you can't afford to buy the item now, *don't get it*. Save and buy it once you have the money. If you can live without a cell phone, that's ideal, but if you have to have it, get the cheapest plan, and deal with not having an iPhone. You will live; in fact, up until the 1990's people didn't even have cell phones. I know, crazy right?

Let's assume you chose the $35 unlimited plan rather than the $80 mainstream plan. You're now saving $45 per month. That's $540 per year and $2,160 in savings over 4 years. Let's apply this to your life cost pillar. You now have $815 in free money. Looking pretty good, but let's keep going.

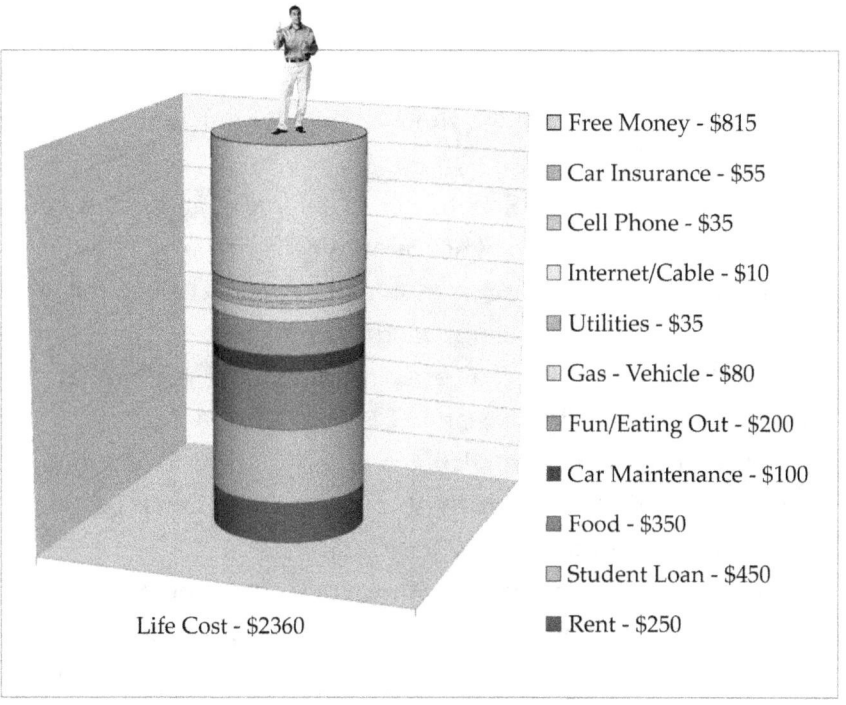

Life Cost - $2360

☐ Free Money - $815

▨ Car Insurance - $55

☐ Cell Phone - $35

☐ Internet/Cable - $10

▨ Utilities - $35

☐ Gas - Vehicle - $80

▨ Fun/Eating Out - $200

■ Car Maintenance - $100

▨ Food - $350

▨ Student Loan - $450

■ Rent - $250

"Money's a horrid thing to follow, but a charming thing to meet." - Henry James

FOOD

I don't know about you but I love convenience, especially when it comes to food. Stopping for fast food is so easy and simple. Going out to dinner with friends is so much more enjoyable than shopping, cooking, and cleaning. When I was paying back my student loans, my choice was to avoid eating out. I still went out with friends, but while they spent $20-$60 on their dinners and drinks, I just got water and hung out. If I was splurging, I would get the cheapest appetizer on the menu. Then I would go home and cook up some pasta. If you've never tracked how much you spend on eating out, I challenge you to do it for one month. You will probably be shocked by how much you spend at restaurants.

There is an expectation for most people that food is food. "Everyone has to eat, so who cares where or how; it's always expensive." That's simply not true. Not only did I shop for what was on sale, I found discount food stores. There was an Amish discount food store with cans of soup for .25 and protein bars for .10. The items were dented, or just about out of date, but I could cut my food budget from $350 a month down to $100 a month. That savings of $250 meant I could pay an additional $3000 per year against my student loans.

Become a coupon clipper. Since you're not going out to the movies as much, you should have time to increase your free money with coupons. There are tons of websites that focus on coupon clipping or combining deals to maximize your food budget. Some people use coupons to shop at the dollar store, get all their food for free, and actually get a refund because the coupons were more than the cost of the food. Sounds crazy, but it's true. Others use coupons and combine them with coupon apps that give rebates. Get creative and aggressive about your food shopping, and see what you can do.

You might say, "But I can't be seen shopping at discount food stores, what would my friends think?" Become a little hippie, and a bit hipster, and tell them you're saving the planet by buying food that would otherwise end up in the dump. I don't care how you explain yourself, or if you explain yourself at all, just buy your food as cheap as you can.

The United States is a country of food waste. The U.S. wastes over 40% of the food produced annually. (For a great resource on this topic watch the documentary, *Just Eat It*.) The food waste crisis is largely because people are more interested in aesthetics than saving money. Stores cannot stock food that is slightly wrinkled or discolored, even if it's perfectly fine to eat. Keep an eye out at grocery stores for food that may be thrown out because it doesn't meet the store's standards. Ask a manager if you can buy the food that was collected, and offer them a fraction of the cost. A lot of stores won't let you do this, but you never know until you try. As for your own food at home, if your leftovers look pretty bad, eat them anyway. I'm not condoning eating moldy or spoiled food, but I am condoning eating the food before it spoils. Keep track of your food very carefully. Make sure nothing goes to waste. Care for your food and it will save you a lot of money on your shopping bill.

All of this may be really hard for some people. I get it; it's no picnic (well actually, picnics are great because they are free. So in a sense you can have lots of picnics, just don't go out to eat). Really, take a vow that you will still hang out with your friends, but refuse to spend money. When I was paying off my student loans, I ate oatmeal for breakfast and pasta or pierogies for lunch and dinner. It was cheap. It wasn't always these three food items, but my meals did rotate around inexpensive foods. A good brown rice can go a long way to extend your food budget. If you need inspiration on cheap food ideas you can always go online. There are entire websites devoted to cheap eating ideas.

Not everyone can eat the same cheap food every day. Perhaps there aren't any discount food stores near you, or you have dietary restrictions. So rather than reducing food down to $100, we will reduce the food cost from $350, which is the national average for one person, down to $200. Anyone who isn't limited by special dietary restrictions and who is shopping smart can eat with $200 per month. This means you're saving another $150 per month. That's $1800 per year and $7200 over four years. Let's look at your life cost. We reduced your food from $350 to $200, which raised your free money to $965. Nice.

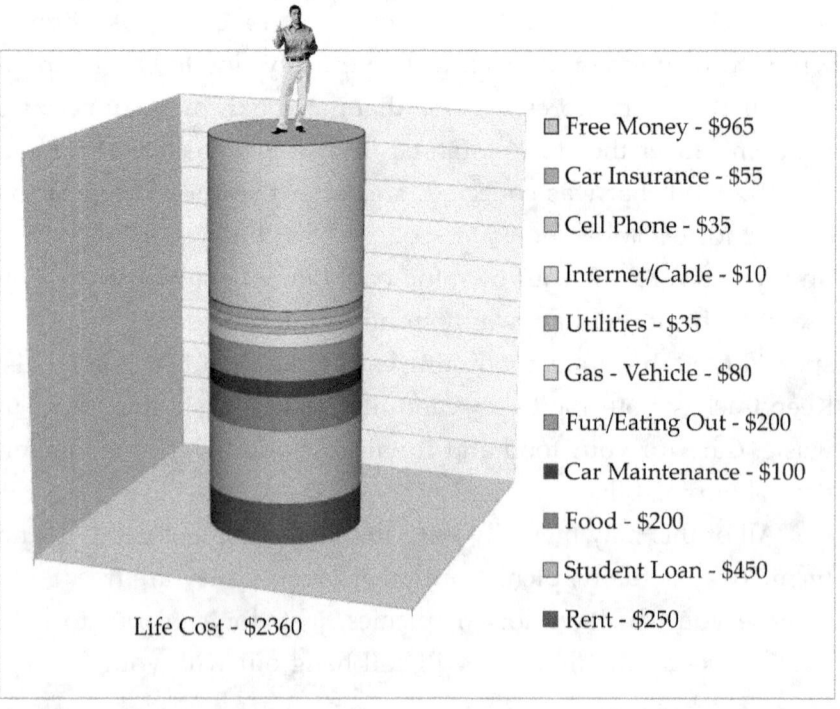

Free Money - $965
Car Insurance - $55
Cell Phone - $35
Internet/Cable - $10
Utilities - $35
Gas - Vehicle - $80
Fun/Eating Out - $200
Car Maintenance - $100
Food - $200
Student Loan - $450
Rent - $250

Life Cost - $2360

"A simple fact that is hard to learn is that the time to save money is when you have some." - Joe Moore

11 FUN/EATING OUT

Everyone has their limit. You can scrimp and save, hold yourself to the highest financial standard, and still feel the need to buy yourself something. You need to go out to eat every once in a while or buy your favorite candy. Maybe you've wanted an iPod for forever, and you're finally earning a salary, so don't you deserve it? The answer is yes! You absolutely deserve it. I still recommend you always ask yourself, "Do I need this to survive?" But sometimes, that answer is yes. Maybe you're really stressed and just need to get fast food. So let's plan for it, so you can do it in moderation. It's better to have some money set aside to let off steam and get yourself something small, then to allow yourself to blow up and go on a spending spree. If you don't allot yourself some fun money, you will probably regret it. However, if you're one of the rare ones, and can do without any fun money, great!

So how much do you give yourself for fun? Right now, it's set to $200 per month. If that sounds like a lot, it's not. It breaks down to $50 per week. That's about enough for one dinner and a movie. Does that mean we increase it? No. In fact, I would challenge you to reduce that amount to $100 or even $50. It means going to the movies is a special treat that you do once a month. You can get fast food, just not multiple times per week. Get creative about how you hang out with your friends. When they want to go to the movies, invite them to play board games instead. Find someone with a fire pit and get marshmallows. Maybe someone you know has a guitar. See what your city has to offer, local art shows, free museum nights, community theater, and street fairs happen all the time. Get old fashioned about how you spend your fun time, and you may realize life can be a lot more exciting than buying the latest video game or watching movies all the time. Then when you really need a night out to see a movie, you have some fun money saved to do it. Or, if you really want that iPod, you save your fun money until you have enough, and then buy it on sale or used.

You may have noticed you don't have a clothing budget. I recommend using your fun money. If you need to go clothes shopping, let's say for your job, go to Good Will or Salvation Army. Then look for their bargain bins; they have shirts and pants for fifty cents each. Another option would be a consignment shop such as Plato's Closet or Threadup.com. You can find great deals on name-brand clothing that are like new. Consignment shops will also sell your old clothing for you. Just drop off your old clothes that you no longer wear. When your old clothes sell you receive a credit that can be used towards the purchase of new clothing. You don't have to use your fun money for clothing, but if you do, it will challenge you to buy sparingly and shop to find those deals.

We will compromise on the fun money and do $75 per month. Let's apply that to your life cost pillar.

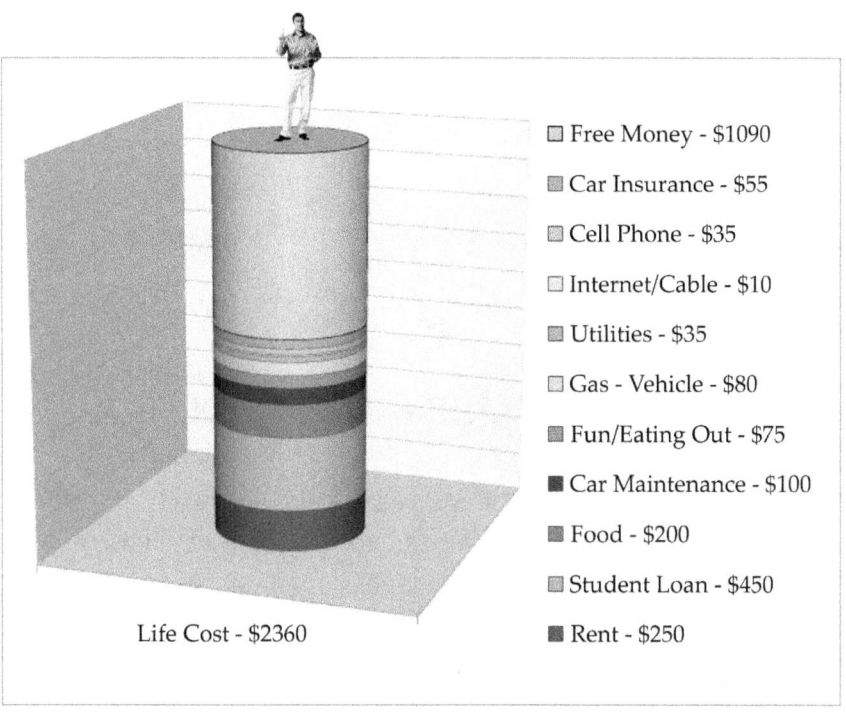

Free Money - $1090

Car Insurance - $55

Cell Phone - $35

Internet/Cable - $10

Utilities - $35

Gas - Vehicle - $80

Fun/Eating Out - $75

Car Maintenance - $100

Food - $200

Student Loan - $450

Rent - $250

Life Cost - $2360

"A penny saved is a penny earned." - Benjamin Franklin

12 HABITUAL SMALL SPENDING

Maybe you enjoy a morning cup of coffee or chai tea. This usually translates to a stop at Starbucks or some other coffee shop. It's a small purchase and very necessary, right? In fact, without joking, most people when asked, "Do I need this to survive?" would answer, "*Yes!*" But a $5 Starbucks adds up fast. $5 per day over 30 days totals $150 per month. That's $1,800 a year in coffee. Free up that money! I'm not saying you shouldn't drink coffee. But buy coffee at a discount food store and make it at home. If it makes you feel better, pour it into a Starbucks cup. This is true for all small spending. What are some daily or weekly purchases you make without thinking? You need to remember that every dollar counts so start thinking outside the box.

THE POWER OF THE DOLLAR

When I was a teenager, I worked for a garage waxing school buses. It was a terrible job, long hours with little pay. Every day, my mind would drift towards my favorite topic; lunch. Lunch was a magical half hour of relaxing, eating, and having a snack. The vending machine called my name, and every day, I bought something different. My parents weren't big on snack foods, especially sweets. So a single dollar would come out of my wallet and bring me a little bit of heaven. One dollar didn't seem like much to me, and my stomach said it was worth it. Then at the end of the month, I looked at my diminished paycheck and wondered what had happened? I didn't make much to begin with, but deduct $30 a month from that already small check, and there wasn't a whole lot left. The same is true for you.

You may not think the soda in the vending machine is a big deal, but it is. Every single dollar reveals your dedication to the question, "Do I NEED that or do I just WANT that?" A $1 vending machine purchase every day means $30 per month. That's $360 per year. It's not just that single dollar; it's the dollar habit. When you think of a dollar as disposable, you take away its value, and you begin to spend one dollar here and another there. Before you know it, you have spent a lot more than a dollar a day. Instead, you need to see every dollar as a piece to your puzzle; every dollar has the power to free you, and every dollar helps to reverse the river of debt. Whatever analogy works for you, use it. Convince yourself to hold onto every single dollar you can get.

The only exception to this rule is if you're using your fun money. Then feel free to buy a soda as a special treat to yourself. Just be sure you understand that the dollar is powerful and do not minimize the compiling effect of the dollar to lower your life cost and increase your free money.

"Advertising is the art of convincing people to spend money they don't have for something they don't need." - Will Rogers

13 SHOP AROUND / ALWAYS ASK

Many people love to shop. They love to find good deals on clothing. This same desire to get a great deal should pertain to all aspects of your spending. When you need to hook up internet, find out if you can get cable, DSL, or cell wireless, and ask for promotional offers. If you call the company directly, they will sign you up at full price. They will never mention that you could save hundreds of dollars signing up through a promotion. So always ask! Ask when getting internet, when ordering a pizza, buying a bed, whatever it is. The first question should be, "Are you running any specials?" If they say no, look online. Most companies offer special deals online that they don't tell you about over the phone. Once, I stepped into a pizza shop and ordered a large one topping pizza for $14. A few minutes later, someone came in and asked for a large one topping pizza for the special price of $10. No coupon, they just asked because they heard there was a deal going on. Sure enough they got their pizza for $10. I was furious; why didn't the pizza guy tell me? He didn't tell me because I didn't ask. So I told him to keep the pizza, and I walked out without paying. A few minutes later, I came back in and ordered the same pizza for $10.

When my wife and I bought our first bed, it was listed as $2,000, but on sale for $1,400. We talked to the sales person and asked for a better deal over and over again. He had to "Check with the manager," which he never did. He just went into the office, held the phone to his ear, and waited for a few minutes before he came out to give us the good news that we could get the bed for $1,000. Sales people always have their tactics, and they will use them all against you. Most of them are trained to charge you as much as possible. We kept asking for a better price until he came down to $800, including a split box spring and mattress cover. Even then, I walked out of the store to go to a competitor with the quote in hand and asked if they would beat it by 10%, and they did. So I took their offer back to the first because, why not ask? We bought the bed for one third of the original price. Did I cheat that company or sales person? Did I hassle or manipulate them? Nope. They would not have sold it to me if they weren't going to make money. If you offer too little, they simply won't sell it. If you don't think you're getting a good enough deal, walk out. You can always come back. Take the best price you can get to a competitor before buying. Compare your purchases with what's available on the internet. It is a powerful tool to get the best deal!

You can download apps on your phone that help find the cheapest gas. Use other apps to collects rebates on food or items you purchase. If you don't have a computer or internet because you cut that cost, go to the library and use their free computers to get the best deals on everything, especially large value purchases and per-month commitments. Take a few minutes and save lots of money.

If you want to rent a movie, go to the library instead. They have a large selection of movies you can check out for free. Always know the resources around you that are free before paying for something. There are many websites out there that focus on coupons and the best deals. If you don't like buying online, print out the best offer and price match it with a local store. If the same item is available at Home Depot and Lowes, one of them will offer you 10% lower than the competitor, so use it!

Don't be afraid to pose the question, "Can you do any better on that price?" or "Is there a discount you could apply to this item?" The worst they can do is say no. When you're shopping and see a scratch or dent, ask for a discount. If you love to make banana bread and find brown bananas at Walmart, ask for a discount on the bananas that are "going bad." Then go home and make banana bread. You can even bring a flyer from another store into Walmart and price match just about anything. It all adds up to free money, so do as much as you can with the time you have.

I can't stand losing money. There have been times when I forgot to pay a credit card or bill, and I was assessed a late fee. It happens to everyone. Most people get really mad, pay the bill, and forget about it. Always ask! Call the company, explain that you never do this, and ask for the charge to be reversed. Some companies won't do it, but most will. If you get a representative that seems reluctant, hang up the phone and call again. Usually the right representative will help you, and it can save you $35 or more in late fees.

A friend of mine lost track of his finances and didn't realize his checking account balance was so low. He had to pay a bunch of small bills and thought the money was there. In the end, he bounced eight checks. His bank charged $50 per bounced check! He called me completely distressed, and I told him to call the bank and ask for the charges to be reversed. Unfortunately, this was the second time this had happened so they refused. Again I say, always ask! Go to the next step. Anyone can call and ask for their money back, so we set up an appointment. I put on my suit, and my friend and I met with the branch manager. I explained that I was his financial counselor, and we were working to get his finances straight. We pleaded for the charges to be reversed, and they budged a little. The obvious effort we showed meant we were serious about getting my friend on track. Their compromise wasn't enough, and I explained his financial situation again. After further discussion, they reversed all of the penalty charges, and we thanked them profusely. You have to be willing to put yourself out there, ask the question, ask it again, and keep going until you get the answer you need. Sometimes this doesn't work, but often it does, and you never know until you try.

"If we command our wealth, we shall be rich and free; if our wealth commands us, we are poor indeed." - Edmund Burke

14 EVERY PURCHASE HAS INTEREST

A good friend of mine had a lot of student loan debt. She was working a consistent job making good money and wanted some financial counseling. So we sat down to talk through a budget. We found as much free money as possible and things were looking promising. She was a sensitive girl and loved animals almost more than people. No really, she cried just looking at animals because she loved them so much. When she said she wanted to get a dog, I grimaced inside and counseled her against it. Animals can be very expensive. She wanted a dog so badly that no matter what I said, it fell within the "I need this to survive" category. So we looked at the price of the dog, the dog food, the vet bills, shots, grooming, and the $35 per month pet fee for her apartment. The total cost would be around $80 per month. She had the money in her budget, but it would cut into her free money and lower her student loan payment. Over the course of a year, she would spend almost $1,000 on this dog. I explained it like this: every large purchase you make, every per-month commitment you make, every small purchase you make, costs you interest. But she was going to pay for the dog out of her income, how would there be interest?

Let's use the yearly cost for the dog, $1,000, as our example. For every $1,000 she owes in student loans, she would pay $70 per year in interest. But with compounding interest she would pay even more. So if it takes her 10 years to pay off her student loan, every $1,000 of her loan would accrue a total of $1,009 in interest. She would literally be paying double by the end of her student loan. But if in the first year, she applied $1,000 against her loan, she would save herself $1,009 in interest!

If she doesn't have the dog, she can pay an additional $80 per month. Since she *would have* put that against her student loans, she is really paying 7% interest on the $1,000, which is an additional $70 per year. The problem is, once that money is spent, she will continue to pay 7% interest on it until her loan is paid off. Why? Because if she had put the $1,000 against her student loans, she wouldn't be paying that 7% so in effect, the dog carries a 7% interest charge until her loans are paid off. If she keeps that dog for 3 years, she will have spent around $3,000 out of pocket on the dog. The first year she will loose 7% of interest savings, which is around $70. By the second year, the dog will have cost $2,000 out of pocket plus the prior year's interest of $70 and the second year's interest of $155 because the interest is compounding. That's a grand total of $2,225 in two years. By the third year, she will have spent $3,000 out of pocket on the dog plus $70 in interest the first year, $155 in interest the second year, and a killer $383 in interest on the third year. In three years, she would spend $3,000 out of pocket and accrued $608 in interest because of this dog. Even if she gives the dog away after the third year, she can't get back the $3,608 she could have put against her student loans. She won't be paying the $80 per month to feed the dog and pay her pet fee, but she will continue to accrue compounding interest on the $3,608 for the remainder of her loan. If it takes her another 7 years to pay off her student loans, she will accrue another $2,273 in interest because of that dog. So how much would that little dog cost her over the course of her 10-year student loan? $3,000 out of pocket, plus a grand total of almost $3,000 in interest! And she would have only kept the dog for 3 years! Imagine the total if she kept the dog for all 10 years. She would have paid almost $17,000 just to have a dog, and that's assuming there are no extraneous vet bills or surgery for the animal.

This is true for any purchase that could instead be put against your student loans. Is it true for food and rent? Yes, technically it's true for every dollar you spend, but you have to eat and have a place to stay, so use this mindset whenever you're considering, "Do I need this to survive?" If the answer is no, you don't need it to survive, then you have to consider, "Do I want this bad enough to pay 7% of compounding interest on it until my loans are paid off? Hopefully, the answer is no. If you think of everything you purchase as having a 7% interest charge for the life of your loan, you may rethink about certain spending, and that is the goal. Your mindset is the key to success.

As for my friend, she bought the dog, which was good for her soul, but not for her life cost or her loans. The decision was hers to make, and sometimes you need to make the decision based on your heart and not your head. Just know there are consequences; weigh them very carefully before deciding. Every decision you make is yours alone. No one is responsible for the way you spend your money except for you. If you know the value of even a single dollar and realize every purchase carries a 7% interest charge, you're on your way to reducing your life cost, finding tons of free money, and paying off your student loans fast.

"Credit buying is much like being drunk. The buzz happens immediately and gives you a lift... The hangover comes the day after."
- Joyce Brothers

15 CREDIT CARDS

Credit cards are often a huge downfall for people. Some financial counselors encourage people to avoid them entirely and shred all of their existing cards. I mostly agree with this. The temptation to buy impulsively and get things you don't need is hard to resist. When you want something, it's so easy to just swipe a piece of plastic. There is a disconnect between the piece of plastic and the actual money being spent. When you pull out the cash and hand it over to the cashier, you see it and feel it. In some ways, it hurts more to see the cash go. Shredding your credit cards also prevents monthly balances, which can accrue high interest charges. Again, if you don't want to carry cash, use your debit card. At least you see the money coming out of your account on your bank statement.

When it comes down to credit cards, know your strengths and weaknesses. If you struggle to avoid "per-month" schemes, or you tend to buy on impulse, get rid of all of your credit cards! If you insist on getting a credit card make sure you follow these guidelines:

1. Pay the card off every month before finance charges are accrued.
2. Only use the credit card to pay for your life costs, not things you want. The only exception is if you have saved the cash ahead of time, and are ready to buy the item outright.
3. Get a credit card that offers a great bonus for signing up; every little bit counts.
4. Get a credit card that offers maximum cash back reward incentives.
5. Set your monthly bills to go through your card to maximize reward points.

"Leave no stone unturned." – Euripides

16 LEAVE NO STONE UNTURNED

It was Halloween, and I was six. Most kids were holding a lunch sized paper bag or a small plastic pumpkin. Not me. I had a full sized paper grocery bag with the top folded down twice to make a handle. Halloween was my favorite time of the year. Dressed as a cowboy and armed with my large paper bag I ran the entirety of our sizable town in one night. It was my goal to hit every single house, never leaving a single piece of candy behind!

Half way through the night, my siblings and I had worked our way to the other side of town. Walking down the street, we saw a house with its light on, the telltale invitation that candy was waiting. As we neared the target, it dawned on us that everyone was passing by this house. Not a single child was in front of or behind us as we walked to the door. Still, we were determined to leave no stone unturned, so we knocked. When the door opened, we were confronted with a house full of nuns. Shock was written all over our faces with a good mix of terror. We weren't churchgoers at the time, but we knew that many churches did not approve of Halloween. If anyone was going to disapprove of celebrating All Hallows Eve, it had to be twenty women dressed in habits living in a convent.

The door swung wide to allow us to enter. We stood in the middle of the room as twenty nuns surrounded us. Rather than seeing stern, disapproving looks, we saw smiles. A tray of hard candy was passed around as they exclaimed how cute we were. Then one nun pulled out a ukulele and the entire convent broke out into a song of "It's a Small World." Stunned did not begin to describe our state of mind. Who would have ever thought we would be dressed in our costumes, surrounded by nuns on Halloween night singing "It's a Small World"? After the song ended, the nuns bid us farewell and thanked us for stopping at their door. We left the convent with huge smiles on our faces, not because of the hard candy, but because of the unique joy shared in that simple song and their smiles. To this day, it is one of my favorite childhood memories, and had we skipped that door like all of the other kids, we would never have met those wonderful ladies.

Sometimes, the door of opportunity is daunting. No one else is opening that door, so why should you? Perhaps it's too much work, or too scary to step out and try something new. The door we are talking about is the one leading you to extra income. You already have a primary occupation, do you need an extra job? Is a part time job worth the additional stress, especially if you're making less than your primary income? The answer is yes. Don't pass it by. Even when no one else wants to open the door to extra income, press forward. Open all the doors you can because you never know when one will lead you to a room full of nuns singing with a ukulele.

"Money won't create success, the freedom to make it will." - Nelson Mandela

17 EXTRA JOBS

My parents didn't have a lot of money growing up, so my five-year-old mind began looking for ways to earn money to feed my budding candy addiction. After the penny tree didn't grow, I began looking for extra jobs. There was a barbershop next door, so I put on my best shorts and walked in and asked for a job. Sure enough, he let me sweep the sidewalk and clean the drains of leaves. Thirty-five cents was my payment, and from that day forward I knew the power of extra jobs. The spring meant cleaning up seeds and twigs, the summer was sweeping, the fall was cleaning leaves, and the winter was shoveling the walk. I approached the local pharmacy asking for a job, but they turned me down. It was a sad day, but I started selling items for school sales and getting prizes instead. My jobs didn't make a lot of money, but it didn't matter because my life cost was already covered. Since my parents paid all of my bills, bought my food, gave me clothes, and provided a roof over my head, all of the money I made was free money. I would love to say I invested that money and earned compounding interest for the next 30 years, but the only thing I invested in was candy.

The point is, you don't have to make a lot of extra money as long as your primary job can cover your life cost. If you normally make $20 per hour, but can only find an extra job for $8 per hour, that's ok. Every hour you work is more free money going towards your student loans. Set your pride aside, and work as much as you physically can.

One of my endeavors at eight years old was making wreaths from grape vines or evergreen trees and selling them. Most of the time, no one bought them, but every once in a while a sympathetic person would buy a wreath, and my candy stash would increase. Get creative about earning extra funds. Go to garage sales and get things cheap so you can resell them on eBay, Amazon, or Etsy. In college, I found my love for computers and taught myself to tear them apart and put them back together. People always need computer help, and I began to make a good side income fixing computers and removing viruses.

Helping a local farmer on the weekend to put in a crop, or biking through the city to deliver packages, could turn into a great way to pay off your debt. Mary Ellen Sheets and her two sons had an old truck, and they were looking for a way to make money. So they put an ad in the paper, offering to haul away trash for the local community. Eventually, they began to get so busy that she bought another truck and hired on 2 more guys. Today, *Two Men and a Truck* have 224 locations in 34 states, and in 2011 had a total of $220 million in sales. She opened the door.

Even helping people for free can turn into paid opportunities in the future. There are always things you can do to make a little more money, and that is the point. It doesn't take much; a few hours a week can add up to hundreds of dollars per month and thousands of dollars per year. You're already above your interest wall, and your life cost is covered so every extra job is powerful free money. And remember, *this isn't forever.*

When my roommates didn't want to mow the lawn, I offered to do it if they paid a slightly higher rent. This time I put the power of per-month in my favor. They paid an additional $20 in rent, which gave me another $60 per month. That's $720 of free money that I put against my student loans every year.

My primary job offered extra income if you became a tour guide. It wasn't overtime, and it didn't pay well, but it was extra money. I could work up to four tours per week. At first, I committed to just one tour per week, but I really dreaded that day. Most of my week did not include a tour, so it made my tour day seem really long. Then I changed my perspective. If my day to day schedule included a tour, I would get used to working those long hours. I committed to four tours a week, and once I got used to it, doing tours didn't seem hard anymore. But on Fridays, when I didn't have a tour, it was a nice break and became really special. When you have the option to work overtime or pick up an extra job, do it as much as possible. After a little while, the additional work will become normal and it won't seem hard anymore. When you don't have to work the extra job, it will make your time off even better.

Numbers became a fun game for me. I know it sounds crazy, but hear me out. Every dollar I saved meant my free money went up by one. Every ten, twenty, fifty, or one hundred dollars I could make in extra income was a little thrill, as I knew my student loans were going to decrease by that same number. I watched as my loans went under $60,000, and I rejoiced. When they went under the $50,000 mark within the same year, I was ecstatic. Paying off my student loan debt became a challenge that was thrilling, because it was working, and I knew I wouldn't be under the weight of debt forever. I wasn't satisfied with paying $500 over my standard payment, I wanted to pay $1,000 or more. So that's what I did. I made sure to reduce my life cost and earn enough free money to pay my full student loan payment plus

$1,000 per month or more.

You have already lowered your life cost as much as possible. On the previous graph your free money was $1,090, but you were only paying $450 per month on your student loans. (Remember, you were on the 30 year plan.) Let's ramp up your payment to the full $700 per month. Since we raised your payment from $450 per month to $700, that means we take $250 from your free money and move it to your student loans. This leaves you with $840 in free money. Let's assume you can earn $200 per month in extra income, because I know you can. We are going to add $200 in extra income to your $840 of free money, which equals $1,040.

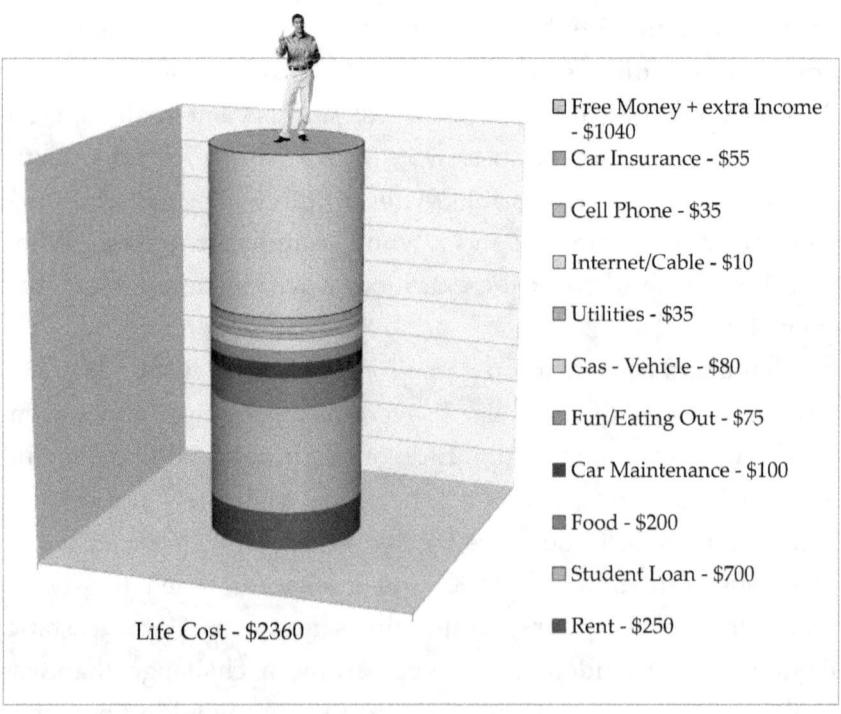

Life Cost - $2360

- Free Money + extra Income - $1040
- Car Insurance - $55
- Cell Phone - $35
- Internet/Cable - $10
- Utilities - $35
- Gas - Vehicle - $80
- Fun/Eating Out - $75
- Car Maintenance - $100
- Food - $200
- Student Loan - $700
- Rent - $250

You did it! In this postgraduate scenario, you're paying the full $700 per month plus an additional $1,000 per month against your student loans! This means you can pay off your student loans in a little over three and a half years! This lifestyle of intense stewardship is for three and a half years, and then you are *free*. It may not be easy, but everything - second job included - becomes normal and day to day once you get used to it. So go after that free money!

"Money can't buy love, but it improves your bargaining position." - Christopher Marlowe

18 IT'S NOT JUST ABOUT YOU

If you're single and just graduated, listen up. It may seem that your student loan is your problem alone. Unfortunately, it's not. If you don't get these loans paid off as fast as you can, they will become your spouse's problem and eventually your children's problem. Will they have to pay them off? No, you will. But it will affect every aspect of your relationships. This may be the biggest and most destructive legacy we leave future generations: a cycle of debt that families cannot overcome. A mindset that debt is just a part of life and everyone is expected to live under its weight.

Money issues are in the top five reasons for divorce. How will an overwhelming student loan payment affect your marriage or your children? Does it mean fewer vacations, no money to spare for a college fund for the kids, more stress around the house on a daily basis? When you carry student loan debt into a relationship or family, you bring along a lot of potential stress. Every dollar you spend and every extra job you turn down could affect your future relationships.

Some friends of mine, Amy and Ray, got engaged during their last year of college. But as Amy came out of college with $140,000 in student loans, Ray rethought the marriage. At least he was honest; he didn't want to start his life with that much debt. Ray wanted to buy a house and start having kids, but that didn't seem realistic with Amy's student loans. The relationship was broken. Let me tell you, Amy and Ray are not alone. It is daunting to enter a relationship with excessive debt, and it can cause a lot of resentment. It made me wonder what prospects I had for a future bride with a $65,000 price tag hanging around my neck.

Get your debt paid off so you can avoid additional stress to your family. Trust me in saying, marriage is wonderful but hard, and there is enough stress without having to worry about excessive debt. Don't wallow in self-pity that you have a large student loan. Pick yourself up and begin lowering your life cost, increasing your free money, and paying off your student loans. Do it for yourself, do it for your spouse, and do it for your kids.

The impact of your financial choices will resound for generations. If you carry debt into your future, it will slow down everyone's financial freedom. If you bring with you a debt free life, the knowledge of how to budget, and the determination to grow your money, you will become financially free and give everyone around you that same freedom.

Everyone wins when you accept the challenge.

"Rule No.1: Never lose money. Rule No.2: Never forget rule No.1."
- Warren Buffett

19 THE CHALLENGE

Remember the river of money I wrote about in the preface? The river is back. Only this time the tremulous waters are being navigated by . . . rats. Yes, that's right, rats, and some of them don't fair very well. (Sorry animal lovers, I don't like seeing animals hurt either. So forgive this example, but it's pretty powerful.)

Curt P. Richter detailed a gruesome experiment in, "On the Phenomenon of Sudden Death in Animals and Man" (191-8). Richter took a rat and placed it into a container of water. The rat began to swim furiously for its life. But after a very short time the rat's head began to dip under the water. A few minutes later, the poor creature sank under the water and died. Richter took another rat, and dropped it into the water. After a short time, the rat began to go under. This time Richter lifted the rat back up, gave it a breath of air, and then released the rat back into the water. Every time the rat began to give up, Richter lifted the poor creature out of the water and gave it a breath of fresh air. After doing this a number of times the rat continued to swim. Richter packed his bags and went home, while the undeserving rat continued to paddle. The next day Richter returned to find the rat was still swimming! He retrieved the brave swimmer from the water, and found the rat to be in surprisingly good health.

What made the second rat swim all through the night, while the first rat died within the hour? The answer is . . . hope. The second rat knew someone was eventually going to lift him out of the water. If he could just keep swimming, he would live.

When the river of money is throwing you around, and the debt seems overwhelming, you need someone to pick you up out of the water. You need someone to give you a breath and remind you that you're not alone. As you re-submerge into the water again you need to be reminded that you don't have to swim this river forever. You need someone to inspire you to hope.

The best way to inspire hope is through "the challenge." You will need someone who is also paying off student loan debt, and ideally, they have a similar situation as you. The amount of debt, income, or living situation doesn't have to be exactly the same. The most important thing is that you're both determined to pay off your debt as fast as possible.

The challenge is to live on the least amount of money possible. You will both be making different salaries, so how much you make, or how much you put against your loans each month isn't the challenge. The challenge is "How low can my life cost go?" If your friend lives on $1,200 per month, can you live on $1,100? When you factor this number, it shouldn't include your student loan payment because you will each be paying a different amount. Instead, this challenge should focus on your food, rent, cell phone, internet, utilities, clothing, fun money, etc. All of the aspects of your life cost that you can control should be added up to compare. You may start with an iPhone and end up with a flip phone. Start with a new car and end up with an older, used car that gets better gas mileage. Challenge each other to reduce, scrimp, and save more. When you think your partner is about to break and needs his or her head lifted up, take a bit of your fun money and celebrate that you're succeeding every month.

The challenge can become fun, as you get creative about new ways to save. Live in a tent in a state forest, work a part time job that gives you free internet and phone; do whatever it takes to spend less than your challenger.

"All I ask is the chance to prove that money can't make me happy."
- Spike Milligan

20 EXPECTATIONS

When I was paying off my school loan, I didn't spend any money. Everyone called me cheap, stingy, miserly, tightfisted, penny-pinching and more. It wasn't easy. Even my family called me these names. There are many reasons why people will pick on you about your lack of spending. Some will be annoyed because you refuse to go out to the movies, others because you choose to take the subway instead of a taxi. Others will feel bad that they are eating a three-course meal at a restaurant while you only get a glass of water or an appetizer. There may be odd or uncomfortable moments because of your lifestyle. Be prepared for it. Don't give in to their pressure. Stand your ground even if they refuse to stand by you.

Remember too, that people don't want you to succeed where they are failing. They often want to drag you down to their level because they are more comfortable with everyone in the same dark place. Remember the war stories we talked about earlier? You can't share bitter war stories about your debt when every month is another success leading you to financial freedom. The tribe mentality will fight to keep you in their ranks. Their comments and name-calling will change one day. That's what happened to me.

One week, I was a stingy, tightfisted, penny pincher; the next week, I sent in my last student loan payment. Everything changed. The same people who called me tightfisted found out I paid off a total of $75,000 in less than four years, and now they called me thrifty. No longer stingy, now I was a good money manager. Before, they were annoyed, and now they looked at me with a fascinated respect. They respected my dedication and asked for help in learning how to pay off their loans. They wanted what I had, and wished they too had walked the harder road and could share in reaping the benefits. Once my goal was accomplished, they saw the wisdom of my frugality.

I hope everyone will support you on your new path. But unfortunately, most of you will get comments and continual resistance. It's time to harden your resolve and expect others to judge you. They will throw out negative comments and try to bring you down. Don't give up; you can do this! Many of those who picked on me are still paying off their student loans, ten years later. In the same timeframe, I paid off my student loans, paid off my first house, purchased a second and third rental property, and just purchased my fourth house. I don't say this to brag, I say it because this system really works.

Eventually, so many people wanted to sit down and talk about my path to paying off my student loans, that I wrote this book. I hope you will find financial freedom from whatever loans you're under. I hope you're inspired to do what it takes.

"It is only through labor and painful effort, by grim energy and resolute courage, that we move on to better things." - Theodore Roosevelt

21 WHAT DOES IT REALLY TAKE?

All change comes from within. No matter how much someone says they want to change, nothing will happen unless they are willing to do what it takes. The skills proposed in this book are not easy. They take sacrifice. But this lifestyle of reduced life cost and creating free money is the key to financial freedom. If you choose to sacrifice now, you will reap the benefits for the rest of your life. You don't have to adopt this as a lifetime commitment, just for a few years to pay off your student loans. However, once you have lived this reduced life cost, you may discover just how much you like saving money. You may find yourself still using these skills even as you loosen up with your finances. No matter how long you employ these skills, your entire life of earning and spending will benefit from your dedication now.

So why not start today? Begin with a mental shift from "I want it now," to "Do I need this to survive?" Once you make the shift, this lifestyle becomes second nature, and I promise it will not feel nearly as hard or sacrificial as you may think. It's just life. Then you need to avoid per-month expenses and really embrace the value of a single dollar. Your life cost has to be lowered, and your free money has to grow. As you step over the interest wall, you can take your free money and make powerful changes in your student loan debt. Hopefully you can use the challenge, so you can walk this road with a friend and be encouraged to save even more, keeping each other motivated to find more ways to save on expenses. Remember, everything you purchase has an interest charge until you finish paying off your loans. Find extra jobs, sell something, and get creative about making money. Prepare your mind for what is to come, and always remember, this isn't forever. The only thing we can control in life is our decisions. By deciding to break free of the burden of debt, by making conscious decisions to sacrifice, you will soon enter a future full of possibility and financial freedom.

"All change is hard at first, messy in the middle, and so gorgeous at the end." - Robin Sharma

WORKS CITED

Amadeo, Kimberly. "What Obama Budgeted in 2016 and What Congress Spent." *The Balance*. N.p., n.d. Web. 14 July 2017.

"Benjamin Franklin Quotes." BrainyQuote. Xplore, 3 July 2006. Web. 27 May 2017.

"Christopher Marlowe Quotes." BrainyQuote. Xplore, n.d. Web. 27 May 2017.

Daily, Investor's Business. "Quotes Of The Day: President Theodore Roosevelt On Progress."Investor's Business Daily. Investor's Business Daily, n.d. Web. 27 May 2017.

"Edmund Burke Quotes." BrainyQuote. Xplore, n.d. Web. 27 May 2017.

"Euripides Quotes." BrainyQuote. Xplore, n.d. Web. 27 May 2017.

Fox, Michelle. "Ten Ideas That Made $100 Million." CNBC. CNBC, 27 Feb. 2013. Web. 15 July 2017.

"George Bernard Shaw Quotations." Richard's Notes. N.p., 26 May 2014. Web. 27 May 2017.

"George Bernard Shaw Quotes." BrainyQuote. Xplore, 4 Apr. 2017. Web. 27 May 2017.

"Henry James Quotes." BrainyQuote. Xplore, n.d. Web. 27 May 2017.

Herbert, Bob. "The Human Cost of Budget Cutting." The New York Times. The New York Times, 19 Feb. 2011. Web. 27 May 2017.

Hernandez, Vladimir. "Jose Mujica: The World's 'poorest' President." BBC News. BBC, 15 Nov. 2012. Web. 27 May 2017.

"32 Inspirational Organizing Quotes." *Good Life Organizing*. N.p., 20 Jan. 2017. Web. 14 July 2017.

"Jimmy Dean Quotes." BrainyQuote. Xplore, 13 June 2010. Web. 27 May 2017.

"Joe Moore Quotes." BrainyQuote. Xplore, n.d. Web. 27 May 2017.

"Joyce Brothers Quotes." BrainyQuote. Xplore, n.d. Web. 27 May 2017.

"Mark Twain Quotes." BrainyQuote. Xplore, 31 Oct. 2016. Web. 27 May 2017.

"Mignon McLaughlin Quotes." BrainyQuote. Xplore, 10 Sept. 2016. Web. 27 May 2017.

"Money Rules of Thumb to Stay in the Green." Tribunedigital-chicagotribune. N.p., 06 May 2010. Web. 14 July 2017

"Nelson Mandela Quotes." BrainyQuote. Xplore, n.d. Web. 27 May 2017.

"Oscar Wilde Quotes." BrainyQuote. Xplore, 2006. Web. 27 May 2017

"Quote By Kevin O'Leary." Quotery. N.p., 24 July 2014. Web. 27 May 2017.

"Ralph Waldo Emerson Quotes." BrainyQuote. Xplore, 8 Sept. 2006. Web. 27 May 2017.

Ramsey, Dave. "The Pain of Change." The Total Money Makeover. Nashville, TN: Nelson Current, 2010. 15. Print.

Richter, Curt P. (1957). On the phenomenon of sudden death in animals and man. Psychosom. Med., 19, 191-8

"Robin Sharma's Blog." Robin Sharma's Blog. N.p., n.d. Web. 27 May 2017.

"Spike Milligan Quotes." BrainyQuote. Xplore, n.d. Web. 27 May 2017.

"29 Warren Buffett Quotes on Investing and Life." Rule One Investing. N.p., 23 Feb. 2017. Web. 27 May 2017.

"Will Rogers Quotes." BrainyQuote. Xplore, n.d. Web. 27 May 2017.

ABOUT THE AUTHOR

So who is Stephen Atherholt? Really, who cares? This book isn't about me, it's about you. It's about the debt-paying, money-handling, powerhouse, formerly-poor-but-no-more . . . you. Now go out there and make a difference in your finances. Then go online, and give the book a good review. Maybe some day you can write me an email telling me of your success. I would love to hear from you. In the meantime, have fun finding free money and kill it. I mean really *kill it*. You can. You will. End of Story.

Email me your story at: Freemoneyforstudentloans@gmail.com

www.ingramcontent.com/pod-product-compliance
Lightning Source LLC
Chambersburg PA
CBHW072040190526
45165CB00018B/1291

* 9 781547 155170 *